Folens
CITIZENSHIP

4

Clea...
issues ... is addressed

OUTBURST!

Mike Gould

Playscripts and drama for CPSHE

© 2003 Folens Limited, on behalf of the author.

United Kingdom: Folens Publishers, Apex Business Centre, Boscombe Road, Dunstable, LU5 4RL.
Email: folens@folens.com

Ireland: Folens Publishers, Greenhills Road, Tallaght, Dublin 24.
Email: info@folens.ie

Poland: JUKA, ul. Renesansowa 38, Warsaw 01-905.

Editor: Kay Macmullan

Layout artists: Suzanne Ward and Patricia Hollingsworth

Cover design: Martin Cross

First published 2003 by Folens Limited.

British Library Cataloguing in Publication Data. A catalogue record for this publication is available from the British Library.

ISBN 1 84303 533 2

# Contents

# Introduction

The plays in this collection, *Law and Disorder*, are designed for use in a conventional classroom, as read-round plays, or for performance in a drama studio or acting space. They have been written so that they work as real dramas, not just as written texts for study, and to that end they are flexible enough to be used, should you or your students choose, as performed pieces in assemblies, or in front of other classes as part of Citizenship work. However, there is no expectation that they are presented like this, and no teacher using them will require drama-teaching expertise.

Realistically, it is most likely that they will be read around a class or group. However, it is recommended that someone (either yourself, or a student) reads the stage directions aloud. For example, a play such as *The wrong face* is particularly dependent on different scenes and locations.

The plays themselves vary in degrees of complexity and length, although it is fair to say that the earlier plays (i.e. the first three or four in the book) are probably more accessible and lighter in tone and subject matter. When writing about matters to do with the law and crime, it is sometimes difficult for the plays not to appear too preachy. This is why certain main characters who could be viewed as bad apples are presented as having redeeming qualities, whether it is Liam in *Reparation*, or Mark in *Ladder*. The most obvious example of this, however, is Tina in *Stolen car*. I also wanted to ensure that the characters are seen as products of their environment, even if, in reality, there sometimes seems to be little motive or reason for their behaviour.

Each play provides basic stage directions, and a character list, and at the back of the book there are brief teacher's notes for each play proposing some discussion points and referring the teacher to aspects of the Citizenship curriculum most suited to the play.

In the end, however, the plays have been designed neither to preach nor to moralise. My task as writer was to create living, powerful dramas that work as good stories. The issues arise out of the decisions and situations characters have to face, not the other way round.

I hope you find the plays stimulating and enjoyable.

*Mike Gould*

# Rules of the game

## Characters

KALEEM: manager, mid-20s

MUSHTAQ: coach, mid-20s

JIMI: goalkeeper

TARIQ: captain

ABDUL: player

JAVED: player

ENIS: goalkeeper

# Scene 1

**Outdoor floodlit pitch. A spring evening.**

*KALEEM and MUSHTAQ watch from the sidelines as other players practise shooting skills. The goalkeeper, JIMI, is not having a good time – several balls go under him, he drops several others, and generally gives an inept performance.*

KALEEM:     It's no good, Mushy. Jimi's useless. We'll be lucky to survive.

MUSHTAQ:   I don't wanna be relegated to Div 3. It's full of headcases. Pub teams and guys who just got out of jail.

KALEEM:     Like you, man?

MUSHTAQ:   That was different. They stitched me up.

KALEEM:     Yeah. Them police officers put all those DVDs in your car.

MUSHTAQ:   They was all white. Once they saw me that was it.

KALEEM:     Anyway, point is – we need a new keeper.

MUSHTAQ:   Easier said than done. Nobody wants to play in goal. Not now. The ground's rock hard.

KALEEM:     Well, if we don't dump Jimi, *we're* gonna be dumped. Into Div 3.

# Scene 2

**The team's dressing room.**

*KALEEM, MUSHTAQ and JIMI sit talking.*

JIMI (*defensive*): I don't wanna play left-back. I like playing in goal.

KALEEM: Thing is, we been leaking goals recently.

MUSHTAQ: Yeah – and we're only two points above the drop zone.

JIMI: Not my fault Abdul can't head the ball.

KALEEM: It's not just that, man. It's you. I mean – you've been a great servant to the club …

JIMI: I've heard those words before. Usually from some Premiership manager before they dump some guy.

MUSHTAQ: It's just, as coaches of the club, we gotta do what's right.

JIMI: So – you kicking me out?

KALEEM: No, 'course not. But we gotta look at other options.

JIMI: Stop talking in code. 'Other options'? You mean someone else in goal.

MUSHTAQ: Nothing's decided. We just need to look at other players.

JIMI (*gets up*): No need, guys. I quit! I'm outa here. (*starts to leave*)

KALEEM: Where you gonna go, man? There ain't any other Asian teams in the league.

JIMI: Well, maybe I'll play for someone else.

KALEEM: Oh, yeah. Downport United, you mean? Yeah, them crazy racist thugs will welcome you with open arms. Or will it be broken bottles?

MUSHTAQ: Why d'you think we set up this club? 'Cos there weren't no teams giving us games.

JIMI: Well, if you don't want me, then I ain't got no choice. (*picks up his kit bag, and moves towards the door*)

MUSHTAQ: We didn't say that.

JIMI: You didn't have to. We'll see how many games you win without a keeper! (*leaves, slamming door behind him*)

*KALEEM and MUSHTAQ sit there speechless for a moment. Then, MUSHTAQ looks at KALEEM.*

MUSHTAQ: That went well.

# Scene 3

*KALEEM and MUSHTAQ with the players, at end of the session.*

KALEEM:    Great, guys. Good stuff. Sit down, if you want to.

MUSHTAQ:    Yeah, it's been a long session.

TARIQ:    What's going on, boss? You never let us sit down. You always tell us to warm down first.

KALEEM:    A manager can change his mind, can't he?

JAVED:    Yeah, what's up? Where's Jimi?

MUSHTAQ:    Calm down. It's cool. It's all sorted.

TARIQ:    What's sorted?

KALEEM:    Jimi … well, Jimi's decided to try his luck elsewhere.

JAVED:    Jimi? No one else will give Jimi a game. Let's face it. He's Asian, and he's useless.

TARIQ:    Come on. He's not Peter Schmeichel – but he's our only keeper.

MUSHTAQ:    Now that's where you come in, Javed.

JAVED:    Me?

MUSHTAQ: I been watching you. You went in goal today, didn't you?

JAVED (*suspicious*):
Yeah, and what's your point, Mushy?

MUSHTAQ: Well, you were good. Kept a clean sheet.

JAVED: I didn't have a shot to save! The only time I touched the ball was taking goal kicks!

KALEEM: Yeah, but them goal kicks were brilliant.

JAVED (*realising what they're up to*):
Hold on, guys. I'm not doin' this! I'm not playing in goal.

KALEEM: I'm the manager. I make the rules.

JAVED: No you don't. Club does.

KALEEM: OK, I pick the team. And you're in goal on Saturday.

# Scene 4

**Watching the match.**

*This scene consists entirely of the reactions of KALEEM and MUSHTAQ to the game. They are standing at the front of the stage, facing the audience. They show various winces and gestures of despair throughout the following.*

KALEEM:    Clear it, you idiot! (*pause*) Get rid of it!

MUSHTAQ:   No – to one of our lot, man! Red shirts.

KALEEM:    Well, pick it up, Javed … I said … No! (*to MUSHTAQ*) What's he doin'?

MUSHTAQ:   Dribbling it.

KALEEM:    You're in goal! PICK IT UP! PICK IT …

*There are several cheers, and then the ref's whistle to signal a goal.*

MUSHTAQ:   Great. Brilliant. 4–0. That's it.

KALEEM:    I thought you said he was good in goal?

MUSHTAQ:   He's got worse, man.

*Ref blows whistle for the end of the game.*

# Scene 5

**Training session.**

*Players are gathered together.*

KALEEM:     Right, guys. We need to work really hard tonight. Put Saturday behind us.

MUSHTAQ:     Yeah, it was a slip-up, that's all.

TARIQ:     A slip-up? They won 4–0. It could have been eight!

KALEEM:     The ref was biased.

ABDUL:     Biased? We didn't have a proper ref. He didn't turn up. It was Tariq's dad.

TARIQ:     Where's Javed?

MUSHTAQ:     Don't know. Anyone got any ideas?

*The players shake their heads.*

TARIQ:     Great. No keeper. And no left-back.

*At this moment, a player starts walking across the pitch. It isn't JAVED, but a different player, ENIS.*

ENIS:     Err. Is this Star United?

KALEEM:     Yeah, man. What is it?

ENIS:     I hear you're looking for a keeper.

MUSHTAQ:     … no, man. You got the wrong team.

TARIQ (*interrupting*):
　　　　　　No, he hasn't! Hands up anyone who
　　　　　　wants to go in goal?

*Deathly silence and no hands.*

TARIQ:　　　See. Come on, Kaleem, give him
　　　　　　a game.

MUSHTAQ:　No way, Kaleem …

KALEEM (*sighs*):
　　　　　　OK, Enis, put a bib on. Show us what
　　　　　　you can do.

# Scene 6

**Pub.**

*TARIQ, KALEEM and MUSHTAQ are sitting around a table. TARIQ and MUSHTAQ have Cokes. KALEEM has a lemonade.*

KALEEM:     Have to admit he's a great keeper.

TARIQ:       Admit? He was brilliant. That save he made from me. I was only five yards out.

MUSHTAQ:   Just a moment, guys. Before, you start offering him a million pound contract, ain't there one little problem?

TARIQ:       You mean what we gonna do to celebrate avoiding relegation?

MUSHTAQ:   No. Bit more serious than that. Ain't you noticed anything about Enis?

KALEEM:     He could catch the ball?

TARIQ:       He bossed the defence around?

MUSHTAQ:   He's white!

*Several other people in the pub turn round and look at MUSHTAQ.*

MUSHTAQ (*to them*):

            What you lookin' at? Ain't you never seen an Asian guy in a pub before?

*They all go back to their drinks.*

KALEEM:     He's from Cyprus.

MUSHTAQ: Not exactly close to Karachi, is it? I mean, think about it. We're an Asian team. We started because we couldn't get picked for white teams.

TARIQ: Things are changing now. Ali's signed on for Moor Park Rovers.

MUSHTAQ: Yeah, but only 'cos his dad owns Moor Park Motors. They sponsor the team. Point is, you remember, we all sat in here. The three of us and Javed. We decided we'd have an all-Asian team. We got to stick to the rules, otherwise …

TARIQ: Otherwise, what? We'll be invaded by white players queuing up to play for us?

MUSHTAQ: Something like that.

KALEEM: Enis is good. With him, we could go all the way. Win the league next year.

MUSHTAQ: Yeah, and where does it stop? Once we're successful we'll be no better than those white cops who pulled me over. Pick and choose who gets in, who doesn't.

TARIQ: It won't be like that. Besides, that rule worked when we started. Don't mean to say we gotta keep it now.

MUSHTAQ: And if Enis had been crap? Would you have been sayin' all this?

*TARIQ and KALEEM are silent. MUSHTAQ gets up.*

MUSHTAQ:    If we're relegated, then we're
            relegated.

KALEEM:     You've changed your tune, man!

MUSHTAQ:    No, I haven't changed. You have.

*MUSHTAQ starts to leave, but at that moment JIMI
enters the pub. MUSHTAQ stops.*

*JIMI comes over.*

JIMI:       All right, guys?

KALEEM *(sheepishly)*:
            Good to see you, Jimi. How's it goin'?

JIMI *(false jollity)*:
            Yeah, great. Fantastic. *(pause)* Actually,
            not great exactly. *(his face drops)* More
            like crap actually.

MUSHTAQ:    What's up, man?

JIMI:       Couldn't get in any teams. Don't know
            if it was 'cos I was crap, or 'cos of my
            skin. They never said. One team said I
            could be third sub.

KALEEM:     Well, that's something.

JIMI *(rounding on him)*:
            No, it's not! It's nothing! I ain't got
            nothing. Our team was all I had. *(with
            difficulty)* You got to take me back.
            Give me another chance.

KALEEM *(awkwardly)*:
            Thing is …

MUSHTAQ: What he's trying to say is, of course you can.

KALEEM: Am I?

MUSHTAQ (*glaring at him*):
There'll always be a place here for you. You were there at the beginning. Remember? All for one, one for all? The first all-Asian team in the league. We made our own rules.

JIMI: So, can I come back?

KALEEM (*to TARIQ*):
What do you think?

TARIQ: I'm keeping out of it. It's your decision, man.

KALEEM: Well, my decision is … half a lager.

TARIQ: Lager?

KALEEM: Yeah, lager.

MUSHTAQ: Lager? You never drink lager. None of us do.

KALEEM: I'm a grown-up. I make my own rules now.

TARIQ: OK, keep your hair on, man!

MUSHTAQ: Lager?

KALEEM: Yeah. That's my decision. I need half a lager. While I think … and give me some space, guys. Please!

TARIQ:     OK, man. It's a difficult decision, and
           you gonna hurt someone's feelings,
           but remember … be brave.

*TARIQ, MUSHTAQ and JIMI all get up and head
towards the bar. KALEEM waits until they've turned their
backs, then crouches down and heads for the door. He slips
out into the street.*

KALEEM (*to audience*):
           I bet Alex Ferguson don't have these
           problems.

# Feel the noise

## Characters

DAVID: late 20s

EMMA: same age, David's wife

PHIL: late 20s

TONY: Phil's brother, mid-30s

# Scene 1

**Night. A small, modern flat, tastefully furnished.**

*The room is dark. In the background we hear, quite
distinctly, the thud and rhythm of loud music. Enter
DAVID, wearing boxer shorts and T-shirt. He switches
the light on.*

DAVID (*calling out*):
  It's just as bad!

*Enter EMMA. She is heavily pregnant. She looks tired and
fed-up.*

EMMA: What? I couldn't hear you because of the
  noise.

DAVID (*snaps*):
  I know why you couldn't hear me. No
  need to say it.

EMMA: No need to snap at me, that's the last thing
  I need.

DAVID (*slumps on sofa*):
  Sorry, love. It's just this noise. How can
  people be so insensitive?

EMMA: We used to play loud music.

DAVID: Yeah. At college. But the flats were full of
  students.

EMMA: Not all of them were into Black Sabbath.

DAVID: I wasn't into Black Sabbath!

EMMA: Deep Purple, then. Or King Crimson. Something with a colour in … wait a minute, (*thinking*) was it … ?

DAVID (*exasperated*):

I don't know who it was! And I don't care! Like I don't care what music that lot are playing. (*gestures at the ceiling*) All I know is I can't sleep, you can't sleep … and when the baby comes …

EMMA: It won't be able to sleep.

DAVID: We're going to have to do something.

EMMA: *You're* going to have do something. I can't confront them. Not in my condition. I might give birth on the landing.

DAVID (*sighs*):

All right. I'll just slip some proper clothes on.

# Scene 2

**The upstairs landing. The music is equally loud
– the same thudding rhythm.**

*DAVID knocks on door. A man, PHIL, answers it. He's
well built, short-haired and well turned out.*

PHIL:      Hallo, mate.

DAVID (*polite*):
           Look, I'm sorry to knock on your door at
           this time …

PHIL:      No probs. I was up. What can I do you for?

DAVID:     It's a bit awkward. It's just … well, the
           music's a bit loud.

PHIL:      Is it? Sounds all right to me.

DAVID:     It's just, it is one in the morning.

PHIL (*looking at his watch*):
           Blimey. So it is. Better be off.

DAVID:     Sorry?

PHIL:      I gotta go. I'm on lates this week.

DAVID:     Oh. So you'll turn it off?

PHIL:      Yeah. 'Course.

DAVID:     It's just … well …

PHIL:      Yeah?

DAVID:     It doesn't matter. I mean, if you're turning
           it off, that's great.

PHIL:     See you, mate. (*shuts door*)

DAVID (*to the closed door*):
          Right. Thanks.

*DAVID waits outside a few seconds. The music stops.*

# Scene 3

**David and Emma's flat.**

*EMMA lying on sofa with her feet up. She has a mug in her hands. DAVID is stood by her.*

EMMA:      Ovaltine. Fancy some?

DAVID:     I'm wide awake now. I could murder a glass of wine.

EMMA:      I think there's some white in the fridge.

*DAVID exits.*

EMMA:      Obviously successful, your visit, then?

*DAVID returns, glass in one hand, bottle in the other. He proceeds to pour a glass and then places bottle on top of cupboard near kitchen door.*

DAVID:     Yes, I suppose so.

EMMA:      Lay down the law, did you?

DAVID:     In a manner of speaking.

EMMA:      What does that mean?

DAVID:     I told him it was unacceptable.

EMMA:      And he didn't hit you, or threaten you, or anything?

DAVID:     No. He was just about to go out.

EMMA:      Go out?

DAVID:     He said he works shifts.

EMMA:      Ah. That explains it.

DAVID:     Does it?

EMMA:      'Course. It's his daytime. Everyone else is
           asleep, he's raring to go.

DAVID:     So, you're saying that level of sound's
           acceptable in the daytime?

EMMA:      No. I'm just saying it explains it. That's
           all. (*takes a sip from her mug*) So he knows
           I'm pregnant?

DAVID (*guiltily*):
           Ah.

EMMA:      David.

DAVID:     I may not have mentioned that bit.

EMMA:      What? You useless great lump!

DAVID:     Well, he agreed to turn the music down,
           so there didn't seem any need.

EMMA:      You know what'll happen, don't you?
           The moment he comes in he'll stick it
           back on again.

DAVID:     He might not.

EMMA:      He will! Don't you know anything? (*with
           difficulty she gets to her feet*) I'm getting
           a drink!

DAVID:     You've had one.

EMMA:      A proper drink. Pass me that bottle.

DAVID:     You're pregnant. It's dangerous for the
           baby.

EMMA:    It'll be dangerous for you if you don't
         pass it to me! Now, give it here.

*DAVID picks up the bottle and passes it over.*

# Scene 4

**The same flat.**

*DAVID is marching out of the bedroom. The music is as loud as ever.*

DAVID:     That's it! Every bloody night this week! I can't sleep, I can't think, I can't … I can't even remember what I can't do! (*marches to door, calling back towards bedroom*) I'm going up there, Emma. This has gone on too long.

EMMA (*in distance*):
                What? I can't hear you!

# Scene 5

**The landing.**

*A different man, TONY, answers the door. He is slimmer and darker than PHIL.*

DAVID:   Oh.

TONY:   Yes?

DAVID:   Umm. Is ... well, I don't know his name ...

TONY:   Phil? My brother.

DAVID:   Err. Might be.

TONY:   He's out. Working.

DAVID:   Shifts.

TONY:   Got it in one.

DAVID:   You, too?

TONY:   Nah, not me. Nine to five. Couldn't stand working nights.

DAVID:   Oh. It's just the music. It's a bit loud.

TONY:   Only way I can relax. Not a great sleeper myself. Find music soothes me.

DAVID:   Yes. I'm sure it does. It's just, well, my wife's pregnant ...

TONY:   Congratulations, mate. Tell her well done from me.

DAVID:   That's not why I'm telling you.

TONY:     You didn't want a baby? Shame, I love
          kids.

DAVID:    Really?

TONY:     Got two of my own.

DAVID:    They're here?

TONY (*laughs*):
          You jokin'? Nah, I left the wife a year ago.
          Moved in with Phil. I couldn't stand it.
          Always crying, always arguing about TV,
          toys, sweets. And that was just me and the
          missus! (*laughs*) Never a quiet moment!

DAVID:    Look, I know you like music. Find it
          soothing. It's just … well, my wife is eight
          months pregnant. It's pretty difficult
          sleeping as it is …

TONY:     She should try playing some music
          – that'd help.

DAVID (*barely holding back his temper*):
          She can hear music. Yours!

TONY:     There you go then.

DAVID (*almost shouting*):
          What I'm saying is – the music has to stop.
          Now. It's too loud!

TONY:     All right. Calm down! No need to shout.
          You'll wake people up.

DAVID:    I have to shout. Because of your bloody
          music!

TONY:      I'll think about it. It's just I don't like your
           attitude. I mean, how would you like it
           if someone knocked on your door in the
           middle of the night, and started accusing
           you …

DAVID (*has now lost it completely*):
           Accusing you? Accusing? Fact: the
           music's too loud. Fact: I asked your
           brother to turn it down.

TONY:      … which he did.

DAVID:     Fact: you turned it up again.

TONY:      You didn't ask *me*.

DAVID:     And … fact: you're a selfish, thoughtless
           thug who if he had any brains would be
           dangerous. Fact: …

TONY:      What did you say?

DAVID:     Oh, didn't you hear? Music too loud?
           Well, I'll repeat it. (*shouts*) You're a selfish,
           thoughtless thug who if he had any
           brains …

TONY:      Right, mate. That's it. (*steps forward and
           punches DAVID*)

*Blackout.*

# Scene 6

**David and Emma's flat.**

*DAVID on sofa, packet of frozen peas over his eye. The music is still in the background. EMMA is stood by him.*

EMMA (*sarcastic*):
>That went well, then.

DAVID (*muffled*):
>I think he knows the strength of my feeling.

EMMA: Yes – you obviously sorted him out.

DAVID: I didn't want to hit him back – he was smaller than me.

EMMA: Very noble of you.

DAVID: Violence solves nothing.

EMMA: You can say that again.

DAVID: I said …

EMMA: I heard you the first time! Look, I think it's time I took charge. We need a twin-track approach … in fact (*suddenly sits down*) Uh-oh.

DAVID (*sitting up*):
>What is it, love?

EMMA: I think you'd better phone the hospital.

DAVID: It's not that bad. Only a black eye.

EMMA: Not you, you idiot! Me! I think the baby's coming.

# Scene 7

**The same flat. Daytime.**

*EMMA opens door. TONY comes in. EMMA has baby, held in her arms. Everything is quiet.*

TONY:    Err, hello. (*stands well back from EMMA and baby*)

EMMA:    Hello, Mr …

TONY:    Roberts.

EMMA:    From upstairs? The one who hit my husband?

TONY:    I was provoked.

EMMA:    Yeah, I feel like hitting him sometimes. Come in.

TONY:    No, it's all right.

EMMA:    Suit yourself. What can I do for you?

TONY:    We had a visit from the council. About the noise.

EMMA:    I phoned them.

TONY:    We've turned the music down now. Me and Phil had a little chat.

EMMA:    Good. I'm grateful. So, what do you want?

TONY:    It's the noise.

EMMA:    Sorry?

TONY: Bit awkward this. (*leans forward and points at the baby*) Her.

EMMA: She's sleeping like a baby. (*laughs at her own joke*)

TONY: She is now. She wasn't at 4 o'clock this morning.

EMMA: No, she wasn't, was she?

TONY: So, what you gonna do about it?

EMMA: Do? What do you want me to do?

TONY: I dunno. Have a word with her. Whatever mothers do to make babies shut up.

EMMA: OK, Mr Roberts. Tell you what. I'll have a little word in her ear. Explain that those nice men upstairs can't sleep. And I'm sure in about a year and a half's time, she'll be nice and quiet, just for you. Goodbye! (*shuts door*)

TONY: Right. A year and a half's time. Wait till I tell Phil. He'll be pleased I sorted it.

# Room

## Characters

JAKE: 18 years old

JOSIE: 18 years old

ROUGHLEY: Mr Roughley, landlord

MANAGER: manager of fast-food restaurant

# Scene 1

**A rented room in a large house.**

*The room should be dingy but have the basic necessities, including sink, wardrobe, etc. It's plain, but OK. There are a few posters on the wall.*

JAKE (*on mobile, sitting on bed in room*):

> Look, Mum, my credit's almost up so I haven't got long. No, it's not Buck House, but it'll do. Yeah, bit dirty, but nothing I can't sort. Well, it's a start. Onwards and upwards, eh? I'll call you soon. When I'm sorted. Say hello to Dad … Love you too. Bye. (*sticks mobile in pocket, and looks around*) Well, they're coming down. (*He stands up and in one sweep pulls the posters off the wall*) Bye bye. (*stands back and admires his work*)

*There's a knock. JAKE opens the door. It's Mr ROUGHLEY, the landlord.*

ROUGHLEY:    All right, son? Getting settled in?

JAKE:    Yeah, thanks. Sorry about the walls.

ROUGHLEY:    What?

JAKE:    You know. The posters.

ROUGHLEY:    Oh, them. Don't matter. Room's yours now. The girl who was in here won't be comin' back.

JAKE: D'you want to hold on to them, just in case?

ROUGHLEY: Nah. Stick 'em in the bin. She mucked me around in any case. Left without paying her last month's rent.

JAKE: Really?

ROUGHLEY: She was just a kid. Didn't know how the big bad world works. But knew enough to con me. (*pauses*)

JAKE: Err … is there something …?

ROUGHLEY: Deposit, son.

JAKE: Oh, right. I thought you said tomorrow.

ROUGHLEY: Today.

JAKE: Right. (*goes to bag, searches for a moment and pulls out a wad of notes*) Here you are. Three hundred and fifty quid.

ROUGHLEY: Four hundred and fifty.

JAKE: The postcard said three hundred and fifty.

ROUGHLEY: It's gone up. After I was mucked around I thought, no more mister nice guy.

JAKE: I don't blame you. I'll get it back, won't I?

ROUGHLEY (*laughs*):
'Course. That's why it's a deposit.

JAKE (*digs into jacket, and pulls out some notes, and some change*):

>Sorry about that. D'you mind the rest in coins?

ROUGHLEY: All worth the same! Right, son. I'll be off. If you need anything, give us a buzz on my mobile – here's my card. I'll be back at the end of the month for next month's rent, all right? (*goes to leave*)

JAKE: Oh, just one thing.

ROUGHLEY (*turns*):

>Yeah?

JAKE: Aren't I supposed to sign something? You know, an agreement or something?

ROUGHLEY: I trust you, son.

JAKE: I know, but …

ROUGHLEY: All right, I'll drop something in tomorrow.

JAKE: It's just …

ROUGHLEY (*impatient*):

>I said I'd drop it in. Now, I gotta go. Got business to attend to. (*exits*)

JAKE (*gets out wallet, and pulls out a couple of notes*):

>Twenty quid. Great. Looks like it's gonna be soup and pasta this week.

# Scene 2

**A fast-food takeaway.**

MANAGER (*closing door*):
    I said we're shut. Can't you understand English?

JOSIE:    They look like foreign students. Probably not.

MANAGER:  No excuse. English is the world language. Everyone should know it.

JOSIE:    Bit harsh.

MANAGER:  It's a dog-eat-dog world out there. I'm doing them a favour. Someone not as kind as me would have ripped them off.

JOSIE:    You do rip them off. You charged that Chinese girl £10 for a burger last night.

MANAGER:  Only 'cos she didn't have any change. Should have been prepared. We're not a bloody travel agents. Right, you, come on – off you go.

JOSIE:    It's payday, isn't it?

MANAGER:  Is it?

JOSIE:    You know it is.

MANAGER:  Right. (*goes behind counter and gets envelope*) Here. Oi, Jamie …

JOSIE: His name's Jake.

MANAGER: Whatever. Where is he?

JAKE: Here. I was just cleaning out the last of those fryers.

MANAGER: Don't want to bother with them. That layer of fat adds to the flavour. There. (*hands JAKE envelope*)

JAKE (*opens envelope*):
Two hundred and twenty?

MANAGER: Yeah. What of it?

JAKE: Aren't I supposed to get the minimum wage?

MANAGER: How old are you?

JAKE: Eighteen.

MANAGER: Yeah, but was your birthday after the beginning of April?

JAKE: Yes. 23 May.

MANAGER: Well, that's it then. You were 17 at the start of the financial year.

JAKE: But I was 18 when I started working for you.

MANAGER: Look, if you don't like it then you know what you can do.

JAKE: That's not right. What d'you get, Josie?

JOSIE: The same.

JAKE:          Well, don't you think it's unfair?

MANAGER:       She's never complained before, so
               don't go putting thoughts in her
               head.

JAKE:          But it's against the law. Even I know
               that.

MANAGER:       Right, that's it! Not goin' to have
               no kid telling me how to run my
               business. (*grabs JAKE and shoves
               him towards the door*) Go on, bugger
               off, and don't bother coming back
               tomorrow.

JAKE:          But, I …

MANAGER:       I don't wanna hear it. (*to JOSIE*) You
               followin' him?

JOSIE *(hesitates)*: I don't know.

MANAGER:       Make your mind up, girl. Clock's
               ticking.

JOSIE (*resigned*): No. It's OK. I'll stay.

*JAKE stands and looks through the window for a moment.
But JOSIE turns away, and moves off stage. JAKE starts
to walk slowly away.*

# Scene 3

**The bedsit.**

*ROUGHLEY and JAKE in Jake's room.*

ROUGHLEY: What d'you mean, you haven't got the rent?

JAKE: Not all of it. I've got three weeks'.

ROUGHLEY (*takes money*):
When can I have the rest?

JAKE: Soon. When I get a job.

ROUGHLEY: That's not good enough.

JAKE: That place you recommended kicked me out. They weren't paying me a proper wage.

ROUGHLEY: You're only 18. Bloody lucky to have something. Got any qualifications?

JAKE (*downcast*): No.

ROUGHLEY: Well then. What you expect? Chancellor of the Exchequer?

JAKE: A decent wage for what I do.

ROUGHLEY: Which ain't anything now, is it?

JAKE: I told you. I'll find something.

ROUGHLEY: And I told you, son. It ain't good enough. (*goes over to Jake's wardrobe and starts stuffing his clothes into a case*)

JAKE:          What you doing?

ROUGHLEY:      Up to you. You can go now. Or I can
               come back tomorrow when you're
               looking for a job and chuck your
               things in the street.

JAKE:          You can't do this!

ROUGHLEY:      Watch me.

*JAKE moves towards ROUGHLEY and puts his hand on
his arm. ROUGHLEY swipes JAKE across the face and
knocks him on to the floor. He throws the last few things
into Jake's case, opens the door and chucks them into
the hallway.*

JAKE:          What about my deposit? And you
               never gave me that contract.

ROUGHLEY:      You lost that when you mucked me
               about with the rent.

JAKE:          You said …

ROUGHLEY:      I know what I said. But that was
               before you conned me. And before
               you tried to assault me.

JAKE:          Assault you?

ROUGHLEY:      Go now, and I'll leave it at that.
               Won't bother to tell the police.

JAKE:          Where am I gonna go?

ROUGHLEY:      I'm sure you'll find some other mug.

JAKE:          I'll be out on the streets.

ROUGHLEY:      My heart bleeds. Now, go on. Get
               out. Before I call the Old Bill.

JAKE:            But I haven't done anything wrong.

ROUGHLEY (*moves menacingly towards JAKE*):
            Do I need to explain myself again?

*JAKE turns, tears streaming down his face, and picks his case up. He looks back one more time at ROUGHLEY.*

ROUGHLEY:    What you waitin' for?

*JAKE exits, half-running, half-stumbling.*

# Scene 4

**A small café.**

*JOSIE and JAKE at a table.*

JOSIE: I'm sorry I didn't stand up for myself. It's just, I need that job.

JAKE: I know. It's not your fault.

JOSIE: What you gonna do?

JAKE: What can I do? Could go back to Mum and Dad's, I guess. Except I haven't got the train fare.

JOSIE: I can lend you a bit.

JAKE: No. I'm not gonna go in any case. It'd be a defeat.

JOSIE: Better than living on the streets. I know. I've done it.

JAKE: I can't face them. Can't tell them I failed. They already blame me for dropping out of school, not getting any exams.

JOSIE: Your mum sounds sweet.

JAKE: She's great. It's Dad. I'm just one big disappointment to him.

JOSIE: So, same question. What you gonna do?

JAKE: No idea. I'm out of money, and I've got nowhere to stay. All I've got left is a few quid on my mobile. Not much use for buying food and stuff.

JOSIE: Well, there is somewhere.

JAKE: Yeah?

JOSIE: It's not exactly the Ritz. But it is a roof over your head.

JAKE: I'm listening.

JOSIE: It's a squat. I know a few guys who are still there. It's pretty rough, but if they accept you, it'll do for a few weeks, till you get yourself sorted.

JAKE: Looks like I don't have any choice.

# Scene 5

**The squat.**

*JAKE sitting on the floor. There's a dirty mattress behind him. There are needles on the floor, and some blankets strewn around. A few crushed beer cans are to one side. There's a bucket in one corner.*

JAKE (*on mobile*):

Hi, Mum. Yeah, it's me. The place? I've moved on. Can't remember the postcode so can't give you the address just now … yeah, it's cool. I've got my own mini *en suite*. The room's kind of minimalist. You know, plain and modern. Yeah. Other flatmates keep themselves to themselves. The job? I'm freelance just now. Whoever pays the most. Yeah, catering. Jamie Oliver better watch out. Look, I gotta go. I'm almost out of credit. Speak to you soon. No, there's nothing wrong. Nothing at all. Everything's just as I expected it. Take care. Say hello to Dad. Tell him … *(with difficulty)* … tell him I'm doing fine. *(stares at mobile for a moment. There are tears in his eyes again. He stands and moves towards the window, which has a narrow shaft of light coming through the boards. He puts his hands on either side of the boards and pulls them together. The light disappears.)*

*Blackness.*

# Wheels on the bus

The following fictional drama is based on the real events that took place in Montgomery, Alabama, in the USA in 1955. Complicated laws required black people to give up their seats on buses, in certain circumstances, to white people. A black woman, Rosa Parks, refused to do so, and was arrested. She became the symbol of resistance to the law and contributed to the surge in civil rights activity that followed, led by Martin Luther King, amongst others.

The characters in the following play are not based on anyone living or dead, although the girl who calls out from the crowd did exist.

## Characters

CASSIE: Cassie Beacon, 8 years old

JULIUS: Julius Beacon, 6 years old

MRS BEACON: their mother

MR BEACON: their father

BECKY: Becky Williams, Cassie's friend, also 8

ABE: Abe Williams, Becky's twin brother, 8

GIRL IN CROWD

# Scene 1

**A relatively humble one-storey house in a suburb of Montgomery, USA. The year is 1955.**

*CASSIE and her brother JULIUS come running up the steps on to the veranda and into the house.*

CASSIE:        Mama! Mama!

*MRS BEACON is in the sitting room, which is in reality a side-room to the kitchen. She is sitting at a table writing a letter. She looks up at the arrival of the children.*

MRS BEACON:    Cassie, whatever is all this fuss about? Put your school-bag down and then come and speak to me. And, Julius, will you look at your shoes?

JULIUS (*looks down without understanding*):
        My shoes?

*MRS BEACON gives a meaningful look across the bare wood floor towards the door. There are large muddy footprints.*

JULIUS:        We was catching spiders in the grass.

MRS BEACON:    Looks like you caught more than spiders, young man.

*JULIUS stands stock still, afraid to move in any direction for fear of making more marks.*

MRS BEACON: (*stands and walks over to JULIUS, unties his shoes and removes them*):
        There!

*JULIUS runs off into the kitchen.*

CASSIE:          Mama! Will you listen now?

MRS BEACON:  Of course. I've been listening all
                the while.

CASSIE:          This is important!

MRS BEACON:  Go on, child.

CASSIE (*the following comes out like a torrent of
excited words, leaping over each other, almost without
punctuation or pause*):
                School says that we mustn't get the
                bus 'cos there was this note that
                we got given and I lost it but I read
                it and in any case you can check
                with Abe and Becky they said that
                we mustn't get the bus 'cos it's not
                right that negroes have to
                do different …

MRS BEACON (*interrupting*):
                Whoaa there, lady …

CASSIE (*continuing*):
                … but we can walk or get a cab.

JULIUS (*re-emerging from kitchen with huge glass
of water*):
                What's a cab?

CASSIE (*exasperated*):
                Oh, Julius! Don't you know
                anything! Like a car, but you pay
                for it.

JULIUS:          Like a bus?

CASSIE:            No! You can't get the bus. School
                   said.

MRS BEACON *(sharply)*:
                   Children! Settle down!

*JULIUS stops glugging from his glass. CASSIE stands,
shifting her gaze from her mother to her brother, still
bursting to speak, hopping from one foot to another.*

MRS BEACON:        You want to go
                   somewhere, Cassie?

CASSIE:            No! We can't go nowhere! School
                   said …

MRS BEACON:        OK, OK. I got the message! Right,
                   Julius, take your glass out. I need to
                   speak to your sister.

*JULIUS turns and goes, slowly.*

MRS BEACON *(gestures at chair)*:
                   Sit down, Cassie, before I nail you
                   to that chair.

CASSIE:            Yes, Mama.

MRS BEACON *(soothing)*:
                   I know all about the letter.

CASSIE:            You do?

MRS BEACON:        Yes. I got a visit from your cousin
                   Arlene this morning. She told me.

CASSIE:            She did? About the buses and
                   all that?

MRS BEACON:        Yes. About the buses and all that.

CASSIE: What we gonna do, Mama? Are we goin' to school, or stayin' at home like they want us to?

MRS BEACON: Hush, child! You, me, Julius and Papa are all gonna sit down and talk about this thing. This is a big thing, girl, and we need to treat it right. And it don't do no good to rush. So, put your school-books away, get yourself a drink and a cookie, and then we'll sit down and talk.

# Scene 2

**Outside the house. The following Monday.**

*MR BEACON is getting on to his bicycle.*
*MRS BEACON is stood on the porch.*

MR BEACON:      Would be nice to support them.

MRS BEACON:     We're not gonna change our
                routine. You've always taken your
                bike. Ain't no sense in taking a cab
                five blocks.

MR BEACON:      And the kids? They'll be OK? Looks
                like rain.

MRS BEACON:     That's why *we're* gonna take a cab.
                Julius doesn't know what's goin'
                on. It's just a big adventure. It's
                like the fair came to town. But our
                Cassie's ready to fight the governor
                himself, if it came to it!

MR BEACON:      I don't want no trouble here. It's
                always been kinda peaceful. Not
                like downtown.

MRS BEACON:     Everything'll be just fine. You got
                those baloney sandwiches?

MR BEACON (*patting his pocket*):
                Right here.

*MRS BEACON walks down the steps of the porch, and
kisses her husband.*

MR BEACON:     What's that for?

MRS BEACON:    Ain't a wife allowed to kiss her
               husband goodbye?

MR BEACON:     You already kissed me. In the
               washroom.

MRS BEACON:    Then I guess it's your lucky
               day, feller.

*MR BEACON pushes off on his bike and exits, slowly,
wobbling before picking up speed. MRS BEACON watches
him for a while before climbing up the steps. Before she can
get to the top, CASSIE comes rushing out.*

CASSIE:        Mama, mama! There's a bus! Look,
               a bus!

*MRS BEACON turns for a moment.*

CASSIE:        There ain't no one on it!

JULIUS (*has crept up behind them*):
               There's a driver.

CASSIE:        Course there's a driver, silly! But
               there's no Abe, there's no Becky,
               there's no Zeb, there's no Oscar,
               there's no Rita May.

*At that moment, a crowd of children bustle past on the
other side of the road led by two adults.*

MRS BEACON (*waves*):
               You wanna join them, Cassie?

CASSIE:        It's them! The twins, and the others.

MRS BEACON:    Well?

JULIUS:        I want to go in the cab!

CASSIE (*sighing*):

> I'd like to walk, Mama. But Julius wants to go in the cab. And it's only 10 cents.

MRS BEACON:

> OK. We'll go by cab. But we're walking the last bit. OK?

CASSIE:

> OK.

# Scene 3

**Outside the courthouse. Packed with throngs of people.**

JULIUS: I can't see! I can't see!

MRS BEACON: I'll lift you. But not too long – you're gettin' way too big!

JULIUS: I can see! I can see!

CASSIE: I can't!

MRS BEACON: Come over here, Cassie. Look through that gap.

CASSIE: There she is!

*A roar goes up. Rosa appears and walks through the crowd towards the courthouse entrance.*

GIRL IN CROWD: Oh, she's so sweet. They've messed with the wrong one now!

MRS BEACON: Don't she just look fine? Proud. How can it be right that decent people like her … decent folk …

JULIUS: Who is she, Mama? What did she do wrong?

MRS BEACON: She didn't do nothing wrong, child. She just wouldn't give up her seat for some white folks.

JULIUS:      Why not, Mama? That's not polite!
             That's why she's in trouble.

CASSIE:      She's not in trouble! She's a hero.

MRS BEACON:  Don't know about being a hero. She
             looks like an ordinary human being
             to me. Like me or you.

CASSIE:      She's gone in! They've shut the
             door. Will they send her to jail for
             ever? Will they hang her?

MRS BEACON:  Cassie! Whatever possesses you to
             say such things?

CASSIE:      People get hanged. Becky and
             Abe said.

MRS BEACON:  Not for refusing to move on a bus!
             Anyway, if they got any sense
             they'll let her off easy. (*puts JULIUS
             down*) Come on, kids. Showtime is
             over. Let's get home.

JULIUS:      I want to go to school.

MRS BEACON:  No school today, honey.

CASSIE:      Hey, look! There's Becky!

*BECKY comes over.*

BECKY:       What y'all doin' now?

CASSIE:      Nothing, I guess. Mama, can Becky
             come round and play?

MRS BEACON:  I need to speak to her mother.
             She ain't here, is she, child? Who
             brought you?

| BECKY: | Grandpa and Uncle Martin. |
|---|---|
| MRS BEACON: | We gotta get home. I'll speak to your mama then. (*to CASSIE*) I got things to do, child. |

*ABE comes up, looking disgruntled.*

| ABE: | Grandpa says we gotta walk back! I'm done with walking. I'm gonna catch the bus! |
|---|---|
| CASSIE: | Don't you say that, Abe Williams! You can't get the bus! |
| ABE: | I'm tired. And it's gonna rain. |
| CASSIE: | It's not gonna rain. Just looks bad. |
| BECKY: | Come on, Abe. We can all walk together. Pretend like we're on the bus. You can be the driver at the front. |
| ABE: | Really? I always wanted to be the driver. I asked him once if I could. |
| CASSIE: | Asked who? |
| ABE: | The bus driver. |
| BECKY: | What, Mr Meanie? That nasty guy? |
| ABE: | Yeah. I asked him if I could have a go. |
| CASSIE (*open-mouthed in admiration*): | What did he say? Did he report you? |
| ABE: | No. He didn't say nothing. Kinda ignored me. |

| | |
|---|---|
| CASSIE: | Makes sense. |
| BECKY: | I said he was a meanie. |
| CASSIE: | Wouldn't have said that to no white kid. |
| ABE: | I told you, he didn't say nothing. |
| BECKY: | He didn't have to! |
| ABE: | Well, I'm the driver now. And I'm not sayin' anything either. (*proceeds to imitate starting the bus, making engine noises, fiddling with an imaginary mirror, etc.*) |

CASSIE (*draws herself up*):
> Yes. And we'll be all the high-and-mighty white folk. (*imitating*) Excuse me, but I think you will find this is my seat!

*BECKY, ABE and JULIUS all fall about laughing.*

CASSIE (*to JULIUS*):
> I think you will find the back door is the way in, young man.

*JULIUS giggles.*

| | |
|---|---|
| MRS BEACON: | Come on, kids. The wheels on this bus are rolling, so you'd better get on before it leaves you behind. (*starts to walk off*) |
| JULIUS: | Mama! Mama! Wait! |

CASSIE (*still imitating white lady*):

> Come on, Rebecca. You sit next
> to me. Tell me all about your day.
> I want to know all about your
> fine new clothes and your fine
> new books.

*BECKY links arms with CASSIE. ABE is in front, still
pretending to start the bus and fiddle with the controls.*

CASSIE (*to ABE*):

> Come on, driver! We'll be late!
> And I ain't stopping for nobody!

*She gives him a push, and they all set off, walking away
from the courthouse.*

# Stolen car

## Characters

PARAMEDIC: man, early 30s

SANDRA: police officer, late 20s

TINA: girl, about 15

MUM: Tina's mum

STEVE: another police officer

# Scene 1

**An embankment by the side of the road.**

*There is a flashing light off-stage or to the side.
TINA is standing on the embankment with a blanket
round her. She's looking down at the ground. There is a
dressing over her left eye. A policewoman, SANDRA, is
talking to a PARAMEDIC.*

PARAMEDIC: She's all right. The odd cut. No need
for stitches.

SANDRA: She's bloody lucky, silly cow. How
she walked away from that …

PARAMEDIC: They all walked away. Or ran
more like.

SANDRA: Yeah, left her to face the music.
Nice friends.

PARAMEDIC: She's as hard as nails, that one. Not
a word when I was dressing the
wound. Didn't even flinch.

SANDRA: Thanks anyway. Look, I'll see
you around.

PARAMEDIC: No doubt Saturday night. What shift
you on?

SANDRA: Same as this one. Late. Just my luck.
All the TWOCs* and pub fights.


[* TWOC: Taking Without Owner's Consent]

PARAMEDIC: Seizure!

SANDRA: What?

PARAMEDIC: Our little joke. As in 'See ya!'

SANDRA: Hilarious. Yeah, see you too.

*PARAMEDIC leaves.*

SANDRA (*goes over to TINA. Brightly*):
      Right, young lady …

TINA (*looks up. A look of utter contempt*):
      Can I go then?

SANDRA: In a moment.

TINA: I wanna go now!

SANDRA: Look here, young lady …

TINA: Don't give me that crap. You don't own me …

SANDRA: OK. So, what's your mum's name? Where d'you live?

TINA: I'm not telling you.

SANDRA: You have to.

TINA: Why? You arresting me?

SANDRA: That depends.

TINA I haven't done anything wrong.

SANDRA: You've been drinking.

TINA: So what? I wasn't driving.

SANDRA: Who was?

TINA:          Think I'm gonna tell you?

SANDRA:        You might.

TINA:          You're a joke. So, you gonna take me
               back or what?

SANDRA:        We'll drop by the station first.

TINA:          What if I say no?

SANDRA:        Work it out.

TINA:          All right, I'll come. But I want my
               mobile back.

SANDRA:        What mobile?

TINA:          Don't try that one. Have you nicked
               it? You're all bent, you lot.

SANDRA:        I haven't seen it.

TINA:          It was in the car. It was my birthday
               present.

SANDRA:        The car's burnt out.

TINA:          Car? More like a junk heap.

SANDRA:        You were lucky we got there before it
               went up.

TINA (*stares at SANDRA with a scarcely controlled look
of hate*):

               Lucky?

SANDRA:        Another few seconds.

TINA:          You think I care?

SANDRA:        Maybe, maybe not. All I know is, luck
               smiled on you.

TINA:                  When have I ever been lucky? (*her
                      face suddenly crumples. She begins to
                      cry*) You don't know what it means!

*SANDRA moves toward her, sits down next to her and
attempts to put her arm around her.*

TINA (*half pushes her away*):
                      Get off! Just leave me alone!

*SANDRA (gets up and walks down the embankment. She
speaks into her walkie-talkie*):
                      Hi, Steve. Yeah, I think I'll need to
                      bring her in.

/

# Scene 2

**Interview room.**

*TINA is sat at a table. She's smoking. She finishes the cigarette and stubs it out. There is a half-finished cup of coffee on the table. SANDRA is sitting opposite.*

TINA:    Haven't you got any Coke or something? That coffee's crap.

SANDRA:    We have to drink it. Don't see why you should get special treatment. (*digs in her pocket and pulls out a mobile. Passes it across table to TINA*)

TINA:    Where d'you get it?

SANDRA:    Paramedic must have picked it up. He left it here on his way home.

*TINA checks display.*

TINA:    There's no credit left. Bastard must have used it for making calls!

SANDRA:    Least he gave it back. You can check your messages, and then you're gonna have to give it back to me.

TINA:    What? It was a present. From Gaz.

SANDRA:    Your boyfriend? Well, what Gaz didn't tell you is, it's stolen.

TINA:    No way. Gaz wouldn't give me a dodgy phone.

SANDRA:    It was from a set of knock-offs being sold round the pubs.

TINA:      I don't believe you.

SANDRA:  Was there a box?

TINA:      No. He said that's why it was reduced. In the shop.

SANDRA:  I bet he did.

*TINA looks at the phone for a moment and then flings it against the wall. It smashes and falls to the floor.*

TINA (*bitterly*):

I knew it. Knew it was too good to be true. (*looks at SANDRA*) It was his stupid idea to nick that car. 'Just a laugh', he said.

SANDRA:  Gaz's idea?

TINA:      He's such a loser. He picks a car that don't work properly. Steering went straight away but he said he could handle it.

SANDRA:  Know about cars, do you?

TINA:      Don't need to be a genius to work it out when the car's veering all over the road. (*looks at cigarette packet*) Can I have another?

SANDRA:  Why not? It's your life.

TINA (*lights cigarette*):

You think you know me, don't you?

SANDRA:  I've seen a few like you.

TINA:      Yeah? Well, how come I ain't seen you down here before?

SANDRA: Oh, you're a regular, are you?

TINA: Could say that. In fact, I half expected the door to have my name on it. So … what's your story?

SANDRA: Nothing. I just transferred here last week. So, there's no point in my cautioning you? Seeing as you've been down here so much.

TINA: Do what you like. Check my record, too.

SANDRA: What'll I find?

TINA: Nothing. Sweet FA.

SANDRA: I find that hard to believe.

TINA: You wanna know why I got in the car with Gaz?

SANDRA: Go on then.

TINA: Because I wanted to do something for myself. Have some fun.

SANDRA: That's what they all say.

TINA: You don't see, do you? You got it all worked out about me. You're thinking, how does she know her way around? How come she knows all about not having to give her address? She's a right little villain.

SANDRA: It crossed my mind.

TINA: Well, they know me all right, down here.

SANDRA: Do they?

TINA: Yeah, but it's not me that gets in trouble. It's my mum. Funny, isn't it? Usually the other way round. Kid gets in bother, they call her mum or dad. Well, there ain't no point in calling him as we don't know where he is. And my mum's probably already here. In some cell, sleeping off whatever she's got pissed on. Yeah, by now she's usually been picked up for something or other. Abusing an officer while under the influence. Or whatever.

SANDRA: So you come down here to help her out?

TINA: I pour her into a taxi, or a bus, and take her home. Promise to keep an eye on her. But I can't do it all the time.

SANDRA: Then Gaz comes round and offers you a bit of relaxation, so you jump at the chance.

TINA: Something like that.

*There is a knock at the door. STEVE, another officer, comes in.*

STEVE: There's someone to see you, Tina.

*Enter Tina's MUM. She's sober.*

MUM: Hi, darling.

TINA: Get away from me. You drunk?

MUM: Don't be silly, love.

TINA: That's a first time then.

MUM: Don't be like that. They called me. Said you were in a spot of trouble.

TINA:     Nothing I can't handle.

MUM *moves towards* TINA.

TINA:     Don't you come near me. I just wanted one night free of you.

MUM:      You don't mean that.

TINA:     Don't I? I'm surprised you ain't at some pub or club, drowning yourself in vodka.

MUM:      I was worried about you. When you went off with Gaz.

TINA:     Well, I'm all right, so you can go. Besides, the police want to question me.

SANDRA:  No, it's OK. You can go now.

TINA:     Don't say that. You think I wanna go home?

SANDRA:  Well, it's better than here.

TINA:     Is it? Look, I know the law inside out. There's hundreds of things you could do me for.

SANDRA:  What do you mean?

TINA:     Wasting police time. Assault.

SANDRA:  Assault?

TINA:     When I pushed you away.

SANDRA:  Hardly Mike Tyson.

TINA:     All right then. Driving a car without a licence or tax and under age.

SANDRA:  You weren't driving!

TINA:      How d'you know?

SANDRA:  You told us. Besides, you were in the
         passenger seat.

TINA:      There must be something I've
         done wrong.

SANDRA:  Nothing we can keep you here for.

TINA:      Well, I'm not leaving. Not yet.

SANDRA (*to MUM*):
         I think you'd better go. We'll drop her
         back later.

MUM (*to TINA*):
         Only if you're sure, love.

*TINA says nothing, just turns to one side.*

MUM:      Right, I'll go then.

*Mum waits a moment. TINA still doesn't acknowledge
her. MUM leaves.*

TINA (*to SANDRA*):
         You can keep me here, can't you?
         Overnight. Don't you wanna question me
         about Gaz?

SANDRA:  You'd grass him up?

TINA:      What? That loser. Tell me what you
         wanna do him for and I'll say whatever
         you want.

STEVE:      No need. We got Gaz. Found him on the hard shoulder of the motorway. On someone's bicycle. We're gonna throw the book at him: no licence, twocking, under age, driving while under the influence, theft, riding a prohibited vehicle on the motorway … and I bet he doesn't have his Cycling Proficiency.

TINA:       Can you do him for that?

STEVE:      Probably not, but if we can, we will.

SANDRA:  Right. You're free to go.

*TINA gets up slowly.*

SANDRA:  Want a lift?

TINA:       No. I'm in no hurry.

SANDRA:  Girl your age shouldn't be walking home at this time.

TINA:       Who said I'm going home? (*picks up her jacket and moves towards the door*) See you. Stay lucky. (*exits*)

# Reparation

## Characters

PC DAVISON: police officer

JENNA: Jenna Smith, probation officer

MARY: Mary Baxton, in her early 70s

LIAM: young man, aged 18–19

# Scene 1

**Front room of Mary Baxton's cottage.**

*MARY is seated in an armchair. A police officer, PC DAVISON, and a probation officer, JENNA, are sitting on the sofa. Both are drinking tea.*

PC DAVISON:  Now, only if you're sure, Mrs Baxton.

MARY:  Quite sure. He seems a nice lad, really.

JENNA:  He is. Just a bit weak.

PC DAVISON:  He's been given 100 hours, but I don't expect it'll take him that long to repair the fence, and re-do the borders. He seems quite handy.

MARY:  I'm sure he'll be fine.

JENNA:  Yes, but what about you? After all, it was your fence he kicked down.

MARY:  I'm not naïve. I know he's no saint, but he said in court he was drunk … and he'd taken something … and I believe him.

PC DAVISON:  Doesn't excuse him.

MARY:  No, it doesn't. But from the way he looked when we met, face to face, I think he's pretty ashamed.

JENNA:  He's good at looking ashamed. I wouldn't read too much into that.

73

*A bell rings.*

MARY:         I'm sorry. Will you excuse me?
              I'm needed.

PC DAVISON:   I was just off in any case.

JENNA:        Yes, I've got to go, too. I've a case
              conference at two. Look, I'll be back
              at the end of the day. See how he's
              got on. Any problems, give me a call
              on that number. (*hands MARY a card*)
              I'll leave it switched on.

*PC DAVISON and JENNA leave.*

MARY:         Thank you. Goodbye.

# Scene 2

**The Baxtons' garden.**

*LIAM is straightening a fence post. It's hard work, and he stops to wipe his brow, then goes back to work. Once the post is straightened, he stands back to admire his handiwork.*

LIAM:  Bloody hell! (*goes back to the post and struggles for a few more minutes. Eventually he stands back and looks at it again*) That's more like it.

*He is unaware of the fact that MARY has left the cottage and is standing behind him, holding a can of Coke.*

MARY:  Much better.

LIAM (*turns round, surprised*):
　　　　Mrs Baxton.

MARY:  Much, much better.

LIAM (*sheepish*):
　　　　Yeah, I got it wrong first time.

MARY:  Oh, I didn't mean that. I meant it's even better than it was before. That fence has always been crooked. You did us a favour knocking it down. (*laughs*)

*LIAM is embarrassed about being reminded of his crime, and says nothing.*

MARY:  Here. (*hands him the Coke*)

LIAM (*takes it, and puts it to one side*):
　　　　Save it for later.

MARY:   Thirsty work, out here. My husband
        couldn't manage it once he became sick. I do
        my best, but I think the weeds are resistant
        to treatment nowadays. Besides, I don't like
        all those chemicals.

*An awkward silence between victim and perpetrator.*

LIAM:   I'd better get on. (*picks up a spade*) Thanks,
        like, for the drink.

*MARY turns to go.*

LIAM (*plucking up courage*):
        I could do them weeds if you like. Where
        are they?

MARY (*suddenly attentive*):
        No, it's fine. Stick to the fence.

LIAM:   But I'll be finished soon.

MARY:   Don't worry about the weeds.

LIAM:   But you said …

MARY (*firmly*):
        No, I'd rather you didn't.

LIAM:   Of course, Mrs Baxton. I'll give you a shout
        when I've finished.

*MARY leaves.*

LIAM (*to himself*):

That's bonkers, that is. She's all sweet as pie to me after I've bashed her fence in, then when I offer to do extra, she jumps down my throat! No pleasin' some people. (*leans on his spade, and gazes round the garden*) Perhaps she thinks I'm gonna dig up her prize petunias. I mean, even I can tell a weed when I see one. (*goes back to the fence, and starts digging round the base*)

# Scene 3

**The garden. Later that afternoon.**

*LIAM is swigging from the Coke can. The fence and border look fine. He looks at his watch and sighs.*

LIAM:    Only 3 o'clock. (*saunters across to the other side of the garden. Then, stops by a flower bed. He leans forward*) Ow! (*leaps back, holding his hand*) Bloody nettles! (*goes back to the fence and picks up some gloves and puts them on. Then, he picks up a gardening fork and marches back over to the bed. He digs the fork in and twists it*) Come on. You know you want to! (*puts the fork down and leans forward and grasps the nettle*) Gotcha. (*pulls and pulls. Suddenly, the nettle snaps and he flies backwards, landing on his backside on the lawn*) Now I know why she didn't want me to do the weeding. She didn't want a death on her hands. (*picking himself up*) Right! This is war. (*this time he marches right into the flower bed with the spade, and digs deep into the root of the nettle*) Take that, you ugly git. (*leans forward and this time pulls out the nettle fairly easily. Looks at plants and chants*) Come and have a go if you think you're hard enough! (*surveys the bed*) Ah ha! My next victim … (*takes a step forward, and suddenly stops*) Bloody hell. (*leans forward and pulls a plant towards him*) Bloody hell … (*pulls a leaf off, and steps back on to the lawn*) Well, well, Mrs Baxton. No wonder you didn't want me to go near your precious weeds.

# Scene 4

**Inside the cottage.**

*MARY enters, carrying a tray. It has two empty cups on it. She is surprised to see LIAM, standing by the mantelpiece. He's looking at the black and white wedding photo.*

MARY:  Liam. I …

*LIAM doesn't say anything. He picks up the photo.*

LIAM (*his voice has changed. It's harder*):
　　　　This you, is it?

MARY:  Yes.

LIAM:  And your husband?

MARY:  Yes, that's right. Why?

*LIAM moves towards her.*

LIAM:  'Cos, it looks kinda old. You know – black and white photo. Was it taken in the sixties? Seventies?

MARY (*laughs, a little nervously*):
　　　　Oh no, much earlier.

LIAM:  Yes, that's what I thought. You don't look the hippy type to me.

MARY:  What do you mean?

LIAM:  I'd say you were pretty much your basic sweet old lady. (*comes even closer, uncomfortably close*)

MARY: Look, I don't know what …

LIAM: Yeah. Sweet. Nice. Never been in trouble in all your life. (*turns and goes to the window and looks out*) Not like me. 'Cos I been in trouble from the word go. Didn't grow up in no pretty cottage.

MARY: Neither did I.

LIAM: No, but you're all right now, aren't you? Living alone, with your pretty thatched roof and garden, with its flowers, and its rickety fence.

MARY: I don't live alone.

LIAM: No? No, I guess you're never alone when you're smoking ganja, are you?

MARY: What?

LIAM: Ganja. Grass. Pot. Or do you have your own special OAP name for it?

MARY: Oh.

LIAM: Not so innocent, now, eh? (*puts his hand in his pocket and pulls the leaf out*) 'Mary, Mary, quite contrary, how does your garden grow?' I remember that. Before my mum left with some other bloke, that's what she used to sing to me. Me, a great big boy of three … and she used to sing me that stupid song … Well, I'm glad she did, 'cos I didn't understand it then, but I do now …

MARY: Liam, let me explain …

LIAM:   No. You listen. I got done for kicking down
        your fence. Yeah, I'd had a few drinks. I'd
        even had a smoke. Tell the truth, I don't
        even remember kicking the fence down. Is
        it like that for you? You smoke it so you can
        forget. Forget your hubbie? Dear old hubbie
        who's no longer here?

MARY (*shouting, suddenly*):
        Stop! That's enough.

*LIAM looks at her, hard.*

MARY:   He's not dead. He hasn't left.

LIAM:   Where is he, then? How come I haven't
        met him?

MARY:   You want to see him?

LIAM:   Yeah. Why not? Let's see the invisible Mr
        Baxton. Perhaps he can magically explain
        why half your flowerbed is filled with
        cannabis plants. Perhaps he can explain why
        losers like me get done, when sweet little old
        ladies get away with it?

MARY:   Have you finished?

LIAM:   Yeah … for now.

*MARY walks towards the stairs. LIAM watches her, stays
where he is.*

MARY:   Come on, then. What are you waiting for?

# Scene 5

**The bedroom.**

*A gaunt, pale figure is half-propped up in bed. He is sleeping, breathing lightly, with his mouth open. His hands are crossed awkwardly in front of him. They are twisted, almost distorted.*

MARY:   Come in.

*LIAM saunters in.*

MARY:   There.

*LIAM looks at the figure on the bed. For a moment he's speechless. When he does speak, his voice is a little softer.*

LIAM:   So, that's him. (*edges forward*) He's not …?

MARY:   No. Listen.

LIAM (*goes further forward. Looks at the figure in the bed*):
            He's breathing.

MARY:   Just.

LIAM (*turns and looks back at Mary*):
            What's the matter with him?

MARY:   He's got MS.

LIAM:   What's that then?

MARY:   Multiple Sclerosis. A muscle-wasting disease. He has a few months left, they tell me.

*LIAM looks awkward. MARY goes to the bedside table. On it there is a pipe. She holds it out to LIAM.*

MARY:  Here.

*LIAM holds it to his nose.*

MARY:  Recognise it?

LIAM (*places the pipe back by the side of the bed*): So that's what the ganja's for?

MARY:  Yes. He tells me it's the only thing apart from the prescription drugs that eases the pain.

LIAM:  But why grow it? You can get it anywhere.

MARY:  Can you see me on some street corner?

LIAM:  S'pose not.

MARY:  And it grows so well in the garden. Must be fertile soil.

LIAM:  Yeah, there was heaps of it. Couldn't believe it. So why didn't you tell me about it?

MARY:  It's still illegal, so I'm told.

LIAM:  Yeah, but they don't do you for it now.

MARY:  Maybe not for smoking it. But growing it? Cultivating it?

LIAM:  They wouldn't do someone like you.

MARY:  Perhaps not. But that's not everything. This is a small village. If word got around …

LIAM:  That's why you didn't mention your husband. You knew if I came up here, I'd smell the stuff … tell everyone.

MARY: Well, you were pretty cross.

LIAM (*ashamed*):
I know. I'm sorry about that. Just seems sometimes there's one rule for some, another rule for others.

MARY: I felt like that when Brian got ill. Why me? Why us?

LIAM: There ain't no reason. That's just life, I reckon. (*moves towards the door*)

MARY: Where are you going?

LIAM: Might as well go now. You're gonna tell 'em anyway 'bout how I threatened you and all that.

MARY: No, I won't.

LIAM: You won't?

MARY: I don't want them to remove you.

LIAM: Why not? I would. After what I said.

MARY: No, you've still got work to do.

LIAM: The fence is fixed.

MARY: I know, but there's still all that weeding. Those nettles are absolute brutes.

LIAM: Tell me about it.

MARY: Now, do you fancy a brew?

LIAM (*smiling*):
Yeah. Why not? Long as it's only got tea leaves in it.

# The wrong face

## Characters

VINDA: (short for Aravinda), shopkeeper, Sri Lankan, mid-40s

JANITA: his wife, mid-40s

JOE: 13-year-old boy

MATTY: Joe's friend

MRS FISHER: Joe's mother

JAI: (short for Jayeth), Vinda's brother

# Scene 1

**Night. A corner shop on an estate.**

*JANITA is behind counter tying up unsold newspapers. VINDA enters. He looks distressed.*

VINDA: They've done it again.

JANITA: What?

VINDA: Smashed the light above the shop. Can't see the sign no more. Did you hear anything?

JANITA: You must be joking. What with those joy-riders outside screeching down the road. And I had the telly on.

VINDA: Shop was quiet then?

JANITA: Yeah. A few kids buying football stickers.

VINDA: What did they look like?

JANITA: I don't know, Vin. You know. Kids. They had their hoods up. Look, I'll get on to the police.

VINDA: Police? They won't come. Not for kids.

JANITA: We'll claim on the insurance in any case. Get a crime reference number.

VINDA: Don't bother. I can't get no insurance after last time.

*JOE enters.*

VINDA: I know you.

JOE:      What?

VINDA:  I've seen you before, hanging around.

JOE:      So?

VINDA:  Someone smashed the shop light.

JOE:      You accusin' me?

VINDA:  That depends.

JOE:      I wouldn't come in here, would I?

VINDA:  You might do. So, what do you want?

JOE:      Twenty Silk Cut.

VINDA:  You're too young.

JOE:      Nah. I'm 16. Besides, they're for my mum.

VINDA:  They all say that. Got any proof of age?

JOE:      What?

VINDA:  You know. ID.

JOE:      What you on? I'm not having you tellin' me
          what to do.

VINDA:  Well, I can't serve you then.

JOE:      No need. (*pushes past VINDA and grabs a
          handful of boxes off the shelf. Then holds them
          up as he backs out*)

JOE:      See.

VINDA:  Oi. (*comes round counter after JOE, and tries
          to grab him*)

JOE:     Get off, Paki!

*JOE wrenches himself free, and runs off. VINDA is half-knocked to the ground. As he falls, he pulls down a shelf of biscuits and jars. They lie on the floor around him. He sinks to his knees.*

VINDA:   What are we going to do, Janita?

JANITA:  We have to phone the police.

VINDA:   I told you. There's nothing they can do.

JANITA:  They'll do something this time.

VINDA (*gets up, clutching a handful of broken packets*): Don't you get it? They're too busy. This isn't serious enough.

JANITA:  So – what do you suggest?

VINDA:   I'm gonna get some real help.

JANITA:  What d'you mean?

VINDA:   I'm gonna speak to my brother.

JANITA:  Your brother? That headcase. He's worse than those kids.

VINDA:   Exactly. Give me the phone.

# Scene 2

**A house on the estate**.

*Joe's mum, MRS FISHER, sits at a table. In the background there is a TV turned up loud. There are toys on the ground, and several dirty plates on the table.*

MRS FISHER:  Where you been? You were gone an hour.

JOE:  Getting your fags. Here. (*throws a packet on to the table*)

MRS FISHER:  Where's the change?

JOE:  There weren't none. Price had gone up. Can I have my tea?

MRS FISHER:  There's nothing left. The twins finished it all.

JOE:  *Mum*! I've had nothing today.

MRS FISHER:  What about school lunch?

JOE:  Wasn't hungry then.

MRS FISHER:  Oh yeah? So that's why I had a call from the school asking where you were?

JOE:  I felt ill.

MRS FISHER:  So you didn't go. Well, if you're so ill you can stay in tonight.

JOE:  I'm feeling better now.

MRS FISHER:  Too bad – I'm going out in any case.

JOE: What about my tea?

MRS FISHER: There's nothing in. I can't stock up till I get my money.

JOE: Can't you get a job or something?

MRS FISHER: Cheeky git. How can I, with you three?

JOE: You've got money to go out.

MRS FISHER: When do I ever go out, Joe? When do I get a break? This is the first time.

JOE: And what about me?

MRS FISHER: I'll get you something from the chippy on the way back.

JOE: The chippy? It's the chippy every night.

MRS FISHER: Everybody likes chips.

JOE: I've had enough of bleedin' chips. This is crap. I'm goin' out.

MRS FISHER: You can't.

JOE: Watch me. (*picks up his coat and runs out*)

MRS FISHER: Joe! You selfish little … (*runs to the door*) If you …

*JOE has gone.*

MRS FISHER: Joe! I mean it … (*waits, then turns back into the house. Slams the door. She slumps down at the table. She opens a new packet of cigarettes, and takes one out*)

# Scene 3

**Outside the shop.**

*JOE and MATTY lean against a wall. Matty's bike lies on the ground.*

JOE:        All right?

MATTY:    Nah. I'm bored.

JOE:        Got your mobile?

MATTY:    Out of credit.

JOE:        I got some money.

MATTY:    How come?

JOE:        Mum. She gave it me for helping out.

MATTY:    Your mum? As if.

JOE (*pushes him*):
             What you saying?

MATTY:    Nothing. Just kidding.

JOE:        You'd better be.

*They sit for a few moments.*

JOE:        I'm starving.

MATTY:    I had mine. Pizza.

JOE:        Look, can you go in the shop and get me
             a pie or something?

MATTY:    Why don't you go?

JOE:        Paki in there don't like me.

MATTY: He's not a Paki.

JOE: Don't be stupid

MATTY: He's not. I play football with his son, Lewis.

JOE: Lewis? That's not a Paki name.

MATTY: That's got nothing to do with it. He's Sri Lankan. Lewis was born here.

JOE: You seem pretty cosy with him.

MATTY: I'm not. He goes to football club, that's all.

JOE: Well, you can go in, seeing as you know them and all.

MATTY: I've never met his dad.

JOE: All the better.

MATTY: Why?

JOE: Nothing. Go on.

MATTY: What about the money?

JOE: You won't need it. It's dead easy to nick stuff. Pies are on the shelf just inside the door.

MATTY: No way.

JOE: They can afford it. They're rolling in it.

MATTY: What if Lewis sees me?

JOE: He won't. I saw him go past on his bike.

MATTY: He might come back.

JOE:        Not yet. Go on. Here. Borrow my top – it's
            got a hood on. They won't see you then.

MATTY:      Can't you do it?

JOE:        You scared?

MATTY:      It's not that.

JOE:        You're scared. Always knew you had
            no bottle.

MATTY:      I'm not scared, right?

JOE:        Well then. It's only a stupid shop.

MATTY (*one last try*):
            Just don't know why you can't do it.

JOE:        I told you. They know me.

MATTY:      All right. Just this once. But if there's any
            trouble, I'm outa there. (*takes JOE's top,
            puts it on and pulls up the hood. He walks
            into shop*)

*JOE waits. A few seconds later there's a cry. Then, the
sound of something smashing. MATTY half-staggers out
of the shop. He's holding his head. He falls to the ground.*

JOE:        Matty!

*Vinda's brother JAI emerges from the shop. He's wielding
a baseball bat. VINDA and JANITA follow him.*

JANITA:     You didn't have to hit him! He's just
            a kid.

VINDA:      I thought you was gonna scare him off.

JAI:        I have. He won't come back.

JANITA:     He's hurt bad.

JOE (*running forward*):
   Matty! (*kneels down by him*) Can you hear me?

JANITA:   Call an ambulance.

JAI:   What? For scum like this? You gotta be strong, bruv.

VINDA:   You got the wrong kid.

JAI:   What d'you mean? You said it was him. The one who nicked the fags and smashed the light.

VINDA:   It looked like him.

JANITA (*to JAI*):
   You'd better get out of here.

JAI:   I'm not running off.

VINDA:   She's right. Just go.

JAI:   Aren't you gonna thank me?

JANITA:   What? For almost killing someone?

JAI:   You can't make an omelette without breaking eggs.

JOE (*looking up, urgent*):
   Can't you lot do something?

JANITA (*getting out mobile*):
   I'll phone now.

VINDA (*to JAI*):
   Please go.

JAI:   Right, bruv. But call me if you need me.

JANITA (*phone in hand*):
   The ambulance is coming.

# Scene 4

**Hospital, 24 hours later.**

*JOE by MATTY's bed. MATTY is on a drip. He is unconscious.*

JOE:    I don't know what to say. Not sure you can hear me in any case. It's just everything got all mixed up in my mind. You don't know what it's like in our house. Mum don't know what she's doing half the time. The twins are a nightmare. I have to get out.

I wanna help her, but it's like the moment I come through the door she wants something. I can't even watch the telly without the twins killing each other right near me. So, I go out. I know it's not an excuse. I just don't know what to do.

I look at that Paki shop, I think – they've got it all sewn up. Raking it in. I have to wear crappy trainers. I mean, all that stuff. That shop's always busy. That's why I smashed the light over the shop. I did it on the way back from school. I couldn't believe it. It was dead easy. There were some blokes racing some cars behind the shop, tyres squealing. And there was no one at the front. I was alone. I didn't even need a big stone. I hit it first go. It hardly made a sound. But the light went out. No one would see that sign. 'Vinda's. Open all hours.' It felt good.

It don't feel so good now.

I went back today. There were police cars there and a crowd from the estate. Someone had chucked a brick through the window. The shop was boarded up. All dark inside. Funny thing was, the light was on.

Someone had crossed out the word 'Open' and sprayed 'Shut'. 'Shut all hours.' It's almost funny. But then someone else had sprayed 'Killer' over the boarded up window.

But you're not dead, are you?

*Pause.*

Please don't be dead.

Please, Matty.

'Cos the only killer round here is me.

*JOE buries face in his hands. MRS FISHER appears at the window into the ward. She comes in. Sits down next to JOE.*

MRS FISHER: Come on.

JOE: Where are the twins?

MRS FISHER: I persuaded your aunt to come over. Give us a hand for a few days. You must be starving. Where you been all day? You haven't eaten, have you? I mean, look at the time.

JOE (*distracted*):
Time?

MRS FISHER:  It's 10.30. Tell you what … we can stop at that shop… you know…
(*pauses, realises what she was going to say*)

*JOE looks at her hard.*

MRS FISHER:  It doesn't matter. (*more brightly*) I'm sure we'll find somewhere open.

*JOE stands up and starts to leave, without her.*

MRS FISHER:  There's bound to be somewhere.

*JOE turns to face her.*

MRS FISHER:  You know. Another corner shop.

*MRS FISHER starts to move towards JOE, but something in his face stops her.*

JOE (*bitterly*):  You're right, Mum. Absolutely right. There's bound to be somewhere. You know what they say.

MRS FISHER (*quietly*):
What's that?

JOE:  Open all hours.

*JOE turns, and leaves the room.*

*Fade lights.*

*Fade up lights on MATTY in the bed.*

*Fade up the sound of the heart monitor beeping.*

# Ladder

## Characters

MARK:   aged 18

**A sparse, basic set. A bed, a bucket in the corner. A small window.**

MARK:    First crime, hardly a crime. I nicked a Mars bar from the sweet shop. No, tell a lie, I nicked two – I hadn't had no breakfast that day.

Then the next time, same shop, I took a mag off the top shelf. I used that old trick. Ask the owner for something he'll have to check, or look for. I asked for green ink. But you gotta have alternatives – unusual-sized envelopes, a refill for a pen … whatever. In case they find the thing you ask for straight away. So I got the mag, stuffed it under my jacket then I'm out of the shop, on my bike and whizzing down the side alley, but this shopkeeper must have clocked me, because he's cut through the back of the shop and grabs me as I go past.

He didn't call the police or anything. Just shouted at me, and made me give back the mag. Told me to 'be honest'. So I was – I gave him back what I stole. But I lied, like I lied to you just now. 'Cos I'd nicked something else.

Yeah, money. Leant over the counter and stuck my hand in the till. I knew the right buttons to press. Been watching.

So, then I've got some money, and it has to be spent, don't it? It goes through your fingers so easy. Don't matter how big them coins get, they might as well be sand.

See, first they just give 'em to me, the tabs.
Then, when I needed them to make me feel
better I had to start paying. It started when
we ran out of cars to nick on the estate, and
they put these CCTV things in. You had to
do something. Someone nicked my bike.
Or maybe I leant it to someone. Truth is, I
don't know. Can't remember. But once there
was no bike and no cars, what could I do
for a laugh?

They made me feel better. This bloke
comes out and just hands two to me. Says,
'Here you go. On the house.' And Davie's
laughing like a bloody hyena, like I ain't
seen him laughing for months, so I pop one,
then the other, and then I'm laughing too.
And it's so bleedin' funny. We're standing
there. It's pissing down, with those great
big bloody CCTV cameras watching over
us like metal giraffes, and they can't see
us, 'cos we're too close. Right under them.
We're invisible. I *felt* invisible, too. I didn't
even feel the rain any more.

So, the next time I wanna be invisible again,
but the guy's not around so me and Davie
go looking for him. But this time, he's not
outside, he's at some flat, which is all bolted
up and there's a letter-box or something
and we put our hands through. I ain't got
no money so the hand takes my watch.

Actually it's my sister's watch.

Then, as we're coming down the stairs, there's this geezer at the bottom. Thin, pale. And he asks us for some. He gets some money out. Looks more than the watch, so we hand over a tab or two, then out of nowhere these cops bash us against the wall, and next I know we're down the station.

They give me a list of crimes. Tell me which I did, which I didn't.

Tell me I face months, maybe more for dealing, but they'll drop the dealing charge if I'm a good boy.

By the time I get a solicitor I've made up my mind and I put my hand up for those pirate CDs on the market, the DVD player from that shop on the High Street, and some other stuff.

In court they tell the magistrate I've been co-operative, but she gives me this look like I'm filth and I get six months. Not even suspended. Wham, bam, thank you, ma'am.

So, now I'm here. And I feel like the walls are mountains.

When I was a kid, a long time ago, I saw this programme about this guy who climbed mountains without ropes. Can you believe it? Without bleedin' ropes. One mistake and that's your lot.

Well, I'm climbing without ropes now. But I'm not on no mountain. No way. No, I'm on a ladder. And each step ain't gonna get me to the top, to the summit. No, this ladder goes down. And each step takes me down.

Mars bar.

Dirty mag.

Money from the till.

Nicked car.

Possession.

Dealing.

Make up the rest.

And I don't know how I got on the ladder. Was I bored? Truth is, I just wanted a laugh. That's the best thing I can remember. Me and Davie. Under the CCTV, in the rain. Pissing ourselves laughing. That's as good as it gets.

And now I'm here. And I don't know where the ladder leads.

All I know is, it leads down.

# Teacher's notes

## Rules of the game

**Citizenship:** *Knowledge, skills and understanding 1a, 1b*

This play, like some of the others in this collection, is about how we create our own rules and laws to serve the interests of particular groups, or to enshrine their powers, without necessarily thinking through the ramifications of these rules and codes. In the play, an all-Asian football team is faced with the age-old problem of positive discrimination – do they sacrifice an ideal in the face of excellence?

1) **The play**

   What problem do the coach and manager (Mushtaq and Kaleem) face at the start of the play?

   How do they first of all try to solve the problem? How does this solution backfire – in more ways than one?

   How does the fact that Enis is a Greek Cypriot make the situation even more complicated?

2) **General issues**

   This is a play that springs from racism, initially – Star United only exists because the Asian players faced discrimination. What do students think about the notion of an all-Asian team? Will this help promote or hold back ethnic understanding?

   The play ends with a dilemma for the manager, Kaleem: should he pick Enis, or go back to Jimi, the previous keeper? What would students do in a similar situation?

3) **Writing**

   Ask students to imagine that Kaleem decides to tell Enis he is not wanted at the club. Write the scene at training when Kaleem breaks the news to Enis – include the reactions of various members of the team.

## Feel the noise

**Citizenship:** *Knowledge, skills and understanding 1a, 1c, 1g*

Although this play has a light-hearted feel, its subject – the problem of a noisy neighbour – is far from funny. Disputes far more serious than the one in the play erupt all the time, sometimes leading to tragic consequences with the two warring factions coming to blows, or worse.

1) **The play**

   Why are David and Emma especially cross about the noise from upstairs?

   Why is the man upstairs, Phil, not asleep at night-time?

   How does Emma get her own revenge on Phil and Tony? Why is it especially effective with Tony, given what he said about his own family earlier?

2) **General issues**

   What do students feel about the issue of noise and music: shouldn't people be allowed to listen to what they want, when they want? Besides, can anyone agree on a maximum volume that is acceptable?

   Do students know what action they – or their parents – can take if they are unhappy with the level of noise from someone?

3) **Writing**

   Ask students to imagine they live in a block of twenty flats, housing single people, couples and families. They are on a committee of residents. Write down a ten-point 'Fair Noise' policy, which tries to take into account the lifestyles and attitudes of all the residents. The first point could be:

   ● No music at all between the hours of midnight and 6.00 am.

# Room

**Citizenship:** *Knowledge, skills and understanding 1a*

This hard-hitting play deals with the problems facing a young man who has left his home to try his luck in London. In it he faces two stereotypes: the unscrupulous landlord out to make money at his tenants' expense, and the unpleasant employer, only interested in profit, not the welfare of his staff.

## 1) The play

Jake's problems are increased by the fact that he does not get a Tenancy Agreement from his landlord. How might this have helped him, given what occurs later in the play?

How does Jake's boss at the fast-food takeaway try to trick him over the minimum wage?

## 2) General issues

The difficulties young people like Jake face when they leave home to start a new life in a large city are well known. Where can young people go if they need advice about the rules and laws surrounding work and renting? What, if anything, have students learnt about these laws?

## 3) Writing

Ask students to imagine they work in a drop-in advice centre for young people. What would they say to Jake if he came in and told them he had lost his job and his flat and was living in a squat? Write out the advice in about 100–150 words.

# Wheels on the bus

**Citizenship:** *Knowledge, skills and understanding 1a, 1b, 1i*

This play, set in 1955, as described in its introduction, deals with the 'Freedom ride' and the moment Rosa Parks stood up – or more accurately sat down! – to racial prejudice in the USA. Its subject matter makes quite clear the distinction between rights and laws, and how, in special circumstances, those laws should be challenged and broken. However, the play tries to give the personal perspective of those involved, though not directly, in the events of the day. The characters who appear are entirely fictional.

### 1) The play

What momentous news does Cassie bring home?

What evidence is there, at various times throughout the play, that Julius understands less about the situation than Cassie?

### 2) General issues

To what extent were students aware of the issue of segregation in the USA prior to the late 1950s and early 1960s?

The young reverend at Montgomery's church at this time was to become a national – and international – figure who led the fight against race discrimination. Who was he?

### 3) Writing

The bus boycott was one way of drawing attention to the unfairness of the law stating that black people had to give up their seats, or move to the back of the bus, if there was not sufficient room for white people to sit where they wished. Can students write down any other means (non-violent) that could be used to point out how wrong this law was?

# Stolen car

**Citizenship:** *Knowledge, skills and understanding 1a*

This play presents a familiar story – a stolen car and a young person in regular trouble with the police – or so it seems. It also asks questions about the assumptions we make about people, and the way in which the environments people come from bring them into contact with the forces of law and order.

1) **The play**

   What has happened to Tina at the start of the play?

   What assumption does Sandra make about Tina?

   Who appears to be most responsible for Tina's actions?

2) **General issues**

   Tina seems very well acquainted with police practices, and the rights she has. Is it true that she hasn't broken any laws? What do students know about the laws governing driving and the arrest of young people?

3) **Writing**

   Students should imagine they are Sandra. After Tina has left the police station, Sandra decides to write her a letter giving her some advice on how to deal with future situations such as when her mother has too much to drink. What would Sandra say? Are the police the best people to offer advice and assistance in this sort of situation?

# Reparation

**Citizenship:** *Knowledge, skills and understanding 1a*

The play revolves around the community service being done by a youth who has destroyed a fence. Nowadays, courts have the power in certain circumstances to require convicted people to 'make reparation' to their victims. Sometimes this might be as simple as a letter of apology, or a financial payment in line with the damage or injury caused. In this play, Liam makes reparation to an elderly lady, but in so doing reveals a secret that makes him wonder if society treats everyone equally.

## 1) The play

What does Liam discover when he is doing the weeding in the garden?

Why is he so cross about his discovery when he confronts Mary?

What is the real reason for Mary's unlawful crop?

## 2) General issues

Ask students whether they think the idea of reparation to one's victims is a good idea? How might the idea make things worse for some people? Are there some crimes for which reparation is not a good idea?

What do students feel about the cultivation and use of cannabis for medicinal purposes?

## 3) Writing

Write a short piece (150–200 words) arguing either for or against the legalisation of cannabis. Try to find out sufficient information so that the arguments used are clear and supported by some evidence.

# The wrong face

**Citizenship:** *Knowledge, skills and understanding 1a, 1b, 1g*

There have been many cases of shop owners, particularly ones from ethnic minorities, being targeted by local youths, especially on urban estates. The reasons for such criminal behaviour range from racist attitudes to more general boredom and the desire to 'have a laugh'. The play tries to provide several perspectives and avoid dealing in stereotypes, though the notion of the corner shop that is 'open all hours' is central to the story. It is suggested that the police have proved ineffective previously, but this is in no way a general indictment of police (in)action. Indeed, there are plenty of examples of good practice nationwide.

1) **The play**

    Why does Joe run off rather than stay at home for his mum so that she can go out?

    Who does Vinda call upon to help him protect his shop? What is his wife's reaction to this?

    Why do you think Joe smashed the shop light, and then stole from the shop? Look at his long speech at Matty's bedside.

2) **General issues**

    Some people would argue that Vinda and Janita should sell the shop and leave the area to avoid further bother. Do students think this is the right thing to do?

    Who is to blame for Matty's 'accident'? Should people who claim they are under threat in this way be able to use such force to defend their property?

3) **Writing**

    Ask students to imagine they are the lawyer prosecuting Jai who is facing a charge of grievous bodily harm or attempted murder. Write a speech of 100–150 words attacking his actions and arguing that what he did was unnecessary and wrong.

# Ladder

**Citizenship:** *Knowledge, skills and understanding 1a*

This short monologue is designed to show how petty crime and 'having a laugh' can spiral into more serious offences. However, it also raises the question about whether prison can genuinely help someone, or whether it becomes the catalyst for depression and despair. Questions are also raised about the methods police sometimes use for catching criminals. Is Mark actually dealing? Would he have started dealing if the police hadn't intervened?

### 1) The play

What seems to be Mark's reason for first taking drugs? How does the dealer draw him in so that he becomes dependent on them, and therefore moves on to buying them?

Is Mark guilty of stealing the things he admits to having stolen – the CDs and the DVD player? Why does he say he stole them?

What view does Mark have of his future? Do you feel sorry for him or has he only himself to blame?

### 2) General issues

Were the magistrates right to send Mark to prison given what he had done? How often do students think people who appear in magistrates' courts get sent to jail? (In 1997 10 per cent got immediate custody: Home Office, 2000)

### 3) Writing

Ask students to imagine they are Mark. Write a letter to Davie describing what prison life is like. Try to include Mark's feelings on whether he will offend again when he comes out.